The Making of the Drum

Bob Chilcott

for SATB and percussion

In 1984 I was very fortunate to visit Uganda, where a drum maker made me a beautiful drum with a snakeskin head. I'll never forget sitting in the plane to come home and seeing by chance the baggage handlers loading my drum with incredible respect and care. The drum to them is a living spirit.

The poems I set are a celebration of how that spirit is brought to life. The piece enacts the ritual of constructing the drum, whose component parts are drawn from the surrounding nature—a nature that gives of itself almost sacrificially. We hear how the goat is killed for its skin, how the tree, which bleeds cedar-dark when cut, bestows the drum's body, and how the sticks and rattles are taken, all to begin a new life as companions to the gods, music, and the dance. *Bob Chilcott*

Great Clarendon Street, Oxford OX2 6DP
198 Madison Avenue, New York, NY 10016 USA
Oxford is a trade mark of Oxford University Press

MUSIC DEPARTMENT

UNIVERSITY PRESS

*Commissioned by and dedicated to Michael Smedley and the Oxford Pro Musica
Singers on the occasion of their 20th Anniversary Concert, 22 November 1997*

The Making of the Drum

1. *The Skin*

Edward Kamau Brathwaite

BOB CHILCOTT

* Rub hands together in rhythm (alternatively, use Sand Blocks).

Duration: *c.*12 minutes

In addition to SATB choir, the piece requires 2 Rainsticks, 2 Claves, 1 Shaker, a low-pitched Tomtom played with hard sticks (or a large Ethnic Drum), 4 Sand Blocks (optional) and Marimba (optional). If performance includes Marimba, the Marimba part is available to purchase (ISBN 9780193355378).

Text © Edward Kamau Brathwaite 1968. Reprinted from 'The Arrivants' by Edward Kamau Brathwaite 1973 by permission of Oxford University Press.

* 4 singers clap.

* 4 singers clap.

hope, fur - ther than heaven, that will reach deep down to our gods___ where the thin light

can-not leak, where our stretched hearts can-not leap. Cut the rope of its throat,

* 4 singers clap.

* 4 singers rub hands together in rhythm (alternatively, use Sand Blocks).

2. *The Barrel of the Drum*

round-ed with fire, wound-ed with tools that will shape you. You will bleed,

ce-dar dark, when we cut you;_____ speak, speak, when we touch you.

3. *The Two Curved Sticks of the Drummer*

* Unpitched clipped rhythmic shout.

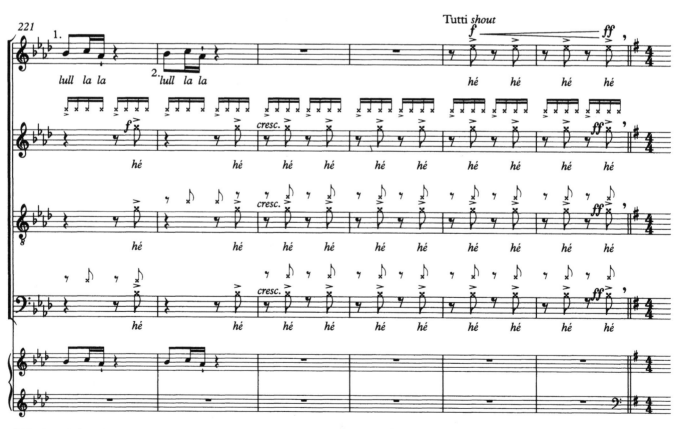

* Unpitched clipped rhythmic shout.

4. *Gourds and Rattles*

* 2 singers clap.

gourd, clash rat - tle, sing gourd,

ca - la-bash trees, ca - la-bash trees, ca - la-bash trees, ca -

trees, ca - la-bash trees, ca - la-bash trees,

gourd, clash rat - tle, sing gourd,

clash rat - tle, sing gourd;

- la-bash trees, ca - la-bash trees, ca - la-bash

ca - la-bash trees, ca - la-bash trees.

clash rat - tle, sing gourd;

5. *The Gong-Gong*

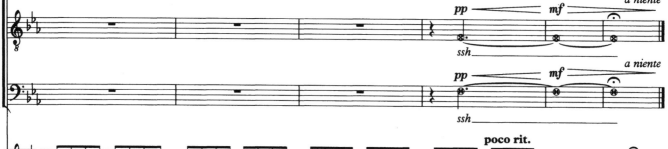

Printed and bound in Great Britain by Caligraving Limited